LIGHT MEALS

Kim MacDonald

Preface

It is necessary to eat special foods in hot weather.
Chilled food is both nourishing and cooling. Surprisingly,
hot, spicy food has the same effect.
Cool, refreshing, tasty dishes should be served in hot,
humid weather or in the middle of a heatwave in order
to stimulate jaded palates and to refresh and feed the
body.
In this book you will find a variety of simple-to-follow
recipes for dishes to serve in summer. Hot weather
catering for the family and friends will no longer be a
problem if you use the ideas in this practical cookery book.

The Editor would like to acknowledge and thank the
following for their kind assistance in providing
props for the photographs in this book.
Incorporated Agencies Pty. Ltd., Sydney
Ban Kura Gift Shop, Cremorne Centre, Cremorne, Sydney
Suomi, Double Bay, Sydney
The Bay Tree, Woollahra, Sydney
Dry Red, 429 Liverpoool Street, Darlinghurst

Frontispiece: Cold Fillet of Beef (see page 34)

This edition first published 1977 by
Octopus Books Limited
59 Grosvenor Street, London W1

ISBN 0 7064 0642 7

Produced and printed in Hong Kong by
Mandarin Publishers Limited
22A Westlands Road, Quarry Bay

Contents

Preface... 6

Weights and Measures............................. 8

Introduction 10

The First Course 12

The Main Course 28

Salads 52

The Dessert Course 68

Cool Drinks 84

Glossary..90

Index 93

Weights and Measures

All recipes are based on the Imperial weights and measures.

Dry ingredients are given in ounces or spoonfuls.
1 standard measuring tablespoon ....20 ml
1 standard measuring teaspoon .... 5 ml

All measurements given are level.

For an accurate spoon measure, level the ingredients off with the back of a palette, French or kitchen knife or with the back of a spatula.

Liquid measurements are given in pints or fluid ounces.

1 pint ....20 fl. oz.

Oven Temperature Guide

Description of Oven	Automatic Electric °F	Gas °F	Gas Mark
Cool	200	200	$\frac{1}{4}$
Very Slow	250	250	$\frac{1}{2}$
Slow	300–325	300	2–3
Moderately Slow	325–350	325	3–4
Moderate	350–375	350	4–5
Moderately Hot	375–400	375	5–6
Hot	400–450	400	6–8
Very Hot	450–500	450	8–10

Introduction

Here is a recipe book you will love to use if you
live in a hot climate or if you have to cope with a
heatwave.

This book gives you ideas for The First Course, The
Main Course, Salads, Desserts and Cool Drinks; ideas
for feeding family and friends throughout a long, hot
summer.

Refreshing ingredients are used in many of the recipes
to sharpen appetites, and contrasting flavours enliven
the taste buds.

Lime juice or lemon juice may be used in dressings for
salads and hors d'oeuvre, in savoury dishes, desserts and
cool drinks.

Other citrus fruit such as oranges and grapefruit and
juicy tropical fruits such as mangoes, pawpaws and
pineapples are served in hors d'oeuvre, salads, desserts
and drinks.

Natural yoghurt with its tangy flavour is used when
making hors d'oeuvre, soups, salads and desserts.

Cool vegetables, salad plants and fruits which are high
in water content are used in many of the recipes; these
include cucumbers, melons, lettuce, radishes, tomatoes
and salad greens.

Use is made of spices, hot chillis, coconut milk,
coconut cream and soy sauce in curries and barbecues
and in some salads. These ingredients add to the flavour,
but also play an important role in cooling the body and
replacing lost natural salt and moisture.

I have tried to keep the cook-housewife in mind when
planning this book by including recipes which require
little or no cooking. Naturally, some of The Main Course
dishes have to be cooked, but these can be prepared in
the cool of the evening, and they require very little
attention during cooking.

Again, in The Dessert Course chapter the only cooking required
is to thicken a custard or dissolve some gelatine. So
you can keep your kitchen as cool as possible with these
recipe ideas, which is most important in summer weather.
All the recipes are easy to follow and the dishes
are simple to make and serve. Food for a hot climate
requires very little garnishing or decoration, but it
should be neatly served and look crisp, appetizing
and refreshing.
With a little thought, planning and organisation, most
of your family's meals may be prepared in advance in
hot weather. I suggest you prepare as much as possible
late at night or early in the morning when the temperature
is cooler, then you too can relax and enjoy the sunshine
in the heat of the day with your family and friends.

The First Course

The First Course, the beginning of the meal, should be small, attractive and appetizing. In hot weather, it should also be very, very cool.

In this chapter I have included recipes for seafood and fruit cocktails, cold fish, vegetable and fruit hors d'oeuvre and chilled spicy soups. These may, in most cases, be prepared well in advance and chilled ready for serving.

An hors d'oeuvre may consist of a single item of food or of a mixture of two, three or more dishes such as pâté with crisp radishes, or slices of hard-boiled egg with dressed zucchini and olives.

Fruit hors d'oeuvre are particularly good, for they are juicy and refreshing and provide a pleasant introduction to a meal, especially in the heat of a tropical night.

Vegetable hors d'oeuvre are light to eat and have a good flavour and interesting texture. They are usually reasonably inexpensive if you use vegetables in season. Dressed with sharp French dressing or vinaigrette dressing, they are delicious.

Hors d'oeuvre, like salads, should be carefully prepared and arranged neatly and attractively for serving. Many may be served in individual glasses, others on small, individual plates.

The term hors d'oeuvre refers most often to the appetizers served with cocktails before a meal. As these can be fairly substantial, the first course is often omitted.

Many of the recipes in this chapter are best eaten as a first course at the table.

Try to tempt the palate with some of these attractive, tasty, chilled first courses on hot summer days. If your family or guests enjoy their first course, they are sure to enjoy the rest of the meal.

Avocado Prawn Cocktail

Avocado Prawn Cocktail

Serves 4

2 avocado pears
8 oz king prawns, peeled
6 tablespoons olive oil
2 tablespoons white wine vinegar
1 tablespoon lemon juice
1 teaspoon sugar
$\frac{1}{4}$ teaspoon dry mustard
$\frac{1}{2}$ teaspoon salt
freshly ground black pepper
$\frac{1}{2}$ tablespoon chopped chives
$\frac{1}{2}$ tablespoon chopped parsley
extra small prawns for garnish

Cut avocado pears in half lengthways and remove stone.
Prepare prawns and place in a bowl.
Place all remaining ingredients, except extra prawns,
in a screw-top jar and shake until well mixed. Pour
dressing over prawns and leave to stand for 10 minutes.
Serve prawns piled in centre of each avocado pear half.
Serve slightly chilled, garnished with extra small prawns.

Melon Cocktail

Serves 4

1 small honeydew melon or canteloup
glacé or maraschino cherries
ground or crystallised ginger
castor sugar or powdered sugar

Method 1: Cut melon into quarters lengthways, remove
seeds. Loosen fruit from skin, cut into cubes and reshape
neatly into a wedge on the skin. Decorate each quarter

of melon with a glace or maraschino cherry.
Serve melon chilled with ground ginger and castor sugar.
Method 2: Cut melon into bite-size cubes or into balls
with a melon-ball scoop. Mix melon with 1 tablespoon
chopped crystallized ginger and place in 4 individual
glasses.
Serve chilled with castor sugar.
Variation: Pour a tablespoon of port over each portion
of melon just before serving.

Cucumber and Pineapple Hors d'Oeuvre

Serves 6–8

1 small pineapple
2 small cucumbers
2 oz blanched almonds
4 fl oz cream
2 fl oz lemon juice
salt and pepper

Peel pineapple and cucumber and cut into ½ inch cubes.
Mix with almonds.
Make dressing by mixing cream with lemon juice. Season
to taste with salt and pepper.
Pour dressing over prepared pineapple and cucumber and
serve chilled.
Note: This hors d'oeuvre may also be served as a sambal
(see glossary) with curry.

Florida Cocktail

Serves 6

3 grapefruit
3 large oranges
castor sugar (or powdered sugar)
2 tablespoons kirsch, optional
6 glacé cherries

Peel the grapefruit and oranges with a sharp serrated knife, making sure all the white pith is removed. Cut the fruit into segments and place on a plate. Sprinkle with castor sugar to taste, and kirsch, if desired. Allow to stand at room temperature for 30 minutes.
Arrange the fruit in individual glasses, pour juice over, and decorate with a glacé cherry.
Chill before serving.
Variation: Dry sherry may be used instead of kirsch.

Mushrooms Milord

Serves 4

4 oz green grapes
4 oz button mushrooms
4 fl oz yoghurt
pinch of sugar

Skin grapes and remove seeds. Wipe mushrooms with a clean, damp cloth and chop finely. Mix grapes and chopped mushrooms with chilled yoghurt and sugar. Chill well. Serve in chilled cocktail glasses.

Mushrooms Vinaigrette

Serves 3–4

8 oz button mushrooms
6 tablespoons olive oil
2 tablespoons tarragon vinegar
1 teaspoon sugar
$\frac{1}{4}$ teaspoon dry mustard
$\frac{1}{2}$ teaspoon salt
freshly ground black pepper
1 tablespoon chopped gherkin
1 tablespoon chopped parsley
1 tablespoon chopped capers

Remove stalks from mushrooms. Wipe mushroom caps
with a clean damp cloth and place in a bowl.
Put olive oil, vinegar, sugar, mustard, salt, pepper
and chopped gherkin, parsley and capers into a screw-top
jar and shake well until ingredients are mixed together.
Pour dressing over mushrooms and allow to stand for 1 hour.
Serve Mushrooms Vinaigrette chilled with slices of French bread,
if desired, to dip into the dressing.

18

Oyster Cocktail

Serves 4–6

2 dozen oysters
shredded lettuce
parsley sprigs and wedges of lemon for garnish
brown bread and butter for serving
Sauce:
4 fl oz cream
2 tablespoons tomato sauce or purée
1 tablespoon Worcestershire sauce
2–3 drops Tabasco sauce
1 tablespoon white vinegar
1 teaspoon anchovy paste
juice of 1 lemon
pinch of dry mustard
pinch of nutmeg
salt
freshly ground pepper

Prepare oysters. Place shredded lettuce in individual
glasses, place oysters on top of lettuce and chill in
refrigerator.
Sauce:
Whip cream lightly and mix in the sauces, vinegar,
anchovy paste, lemon juice, and seasonings. Add salt
and pepper to taste.
Pour the sauce over the prepared oysters. Garnish each
glass with a sprig of parsley and a wedge of lemon. Chill
until ready to serve.
Serve with thin brown bread and butter sandwiches.

Melon with Smoked Ham

Serves 6

1 small melon
4 oz thinly sliced raw smoked ham
freshly ground black pepper
parsley sprigs for garnish

Cut melon into 6 equal segments, remove seeds. Chill melon well.
To serve, place melon on 6 individual small plates.
Lay overlapping slices of smoked ham over each piece of melon and sprinkle with freshly ground black pepper.
Serve immediately, garnished with sprigs of parsley.
Note: Raw smoked ham is obtainable at high quality delicatessen stores.

Melon with smoked ham

Mushroom Liver Pâté

Serves 8–12

4 oz mushrooms, finely chopped
1 oz butter
8 oz cream cheese
8 oz liverwurst
2 tablespoons wine vinegar

Sauté chopped mushrooms in melted butter in a frying pan until golden brown. Drain well, add to remaining ingredients and beat well. Pack mixture into an oiled loaf tin, previously lined with aluminium foil, and chill in refrigerator.
Unmould pâté on to a serving plate and serve with crisp savoury biscuits and accompany with crisp radishes.
Note: Pâté will keep, covered, for several days in a refrigerator.

Tomato Avocado Appetizer

Serves 6

6 large tomatoes
2 ripe avocado pears
3 tablespoons lemon juice
salt and pepper
pinch of chilli powder
6 salted almonds or cashew nuts for garnish

Wash tomatoes and dry with a clean tea towel. Cut a
slice from the top of each tomato and scoop out pulp
carefully with a teaspoon. Turn tomatoes upside down
to drain.
Cut avocados in half, remove seed. Scoop out avocado
flesh and mash to a smooth paste with the lemon juice.
Add salt and pepper to taste and mix in chilli powder.
Season inside of tomatoes with salt and pepper and stuff
with avocado mixture. Chill for at least 1 hour.
Serve on individual plates with a salted nut on each
stuffed tomato.

Iced Tomato Yoghurt Soup

Serves 4

1 pint tomato juice
½ pint yoghurt
1 oz finely chopped celery
1 tablespoon lemon juice
salt and pepper
chopped parsley or chives for garnish

Mix all ingredients together, except parsley, and chill
well.
Serve chilled soup in a bowl sitting in a larger bowl
of ice cubes. Garnish with chopped parsley or chives.

Chilled Tomato Parsley Soup

Serves 4–6

1 lb stewed fresh or canned tomatoes
juice of ½ lemon
1 teaspoon salt
1 slice of onion
parsley sprigs
1 × 15 oz can condensed consommé
2 tablespoons chopped parsley and 1 slice lemon
for garnish

Place tomatoes, lemon juice, salt, onion and a few
parsley sprigs in a blender and mix until smooth and
well blended. Mix tomato purée with consommé. Chill
well. Serve soup chilled garnished with chopped parsley and
thin slices of lemon.

Iced Tomato Juice

Serves 4

1 lb fresh or canned tomatoes
2 teaspoons Worcestershire sauce
1 teaspoon sugar
salt and pepper

If using fresh tomatoes select ripe ones. Place
tomatoes in a blender and mix to a purée. Strain
tomato purée and season juice with Worcestershire sauce,
sugar and salt and pepper to taste.
Serve chilled with an ice cube in each glass or
thinned to taste with iced water.
Variation: Add 1 small finely chopped onion to
the tomatoes before mixing in the blender.

Chilled Chicken Soup

Serves 6

2 × 15 oz cans condensed cream of chicken soup
8 fl oz milk
8 fl oz water
$\frac{1}{4}$ teaspoon dried tarragon
1 carrot, finely grated

Place all ingredients, except carrot, in a saucepan
and heat gently, stirring until smooth. Cool, then
chill in refrigerator for 3–4 hours.
Serve soup in chilled individual soup bowls and add
a little grated carrot to each portion.

Gazpacho

Serves 6

2 lb tomatoes
½ cucumber
1 green pepper
1 red pepper
6 shallots (scallions)
1 tablespoon olive oil
1 tablespoon wine vinegar
8 fl oz chilled water
1 clove of garlic, crushed
salt
freshly ground black pepper
the yolk of a hard-boiled egg for garnish
ice cubes

Remove skin from tomatoes and mix to a purée in a
blender, or press through a sieve with a wooden spoon.
Peel the cucumber and dice finely. Cut peppers in half,
remove seeds and dice peppers finely. Slice the shallots
thinly.
Stir the prepared vegetables into the tomato purée with
the olive oil, vinegar and chilled water. Add the crushed
garlic and season to taste with salt and pepper. Chill
well.
Serve the cold soup in chilled soup bowls. Sprinkle
sieved egg yolk in the centre of each portion and add an
ice cube just before serving.

The Main Course

It is most important in the heat of summer, when
appetites are jaded, to make sure that the Main Course
of the meal is deliciously tempting and looks
refreshing.

The recipes I have included in this chapter include
many cool, nourishing fish and meat dishes. Shell fish
such as crab, crayfish and prawns should be as fresh as
possible, carefully prepared and served with flavoursome
dressings. The dressing may be a rich and creamy
mayonnaise or a sharp and tangy French dressing.

A rich, chilled fish or chicken mousse may also be served
for The Main Course. Accompany it with crisp and
crunchy salad vegetables to add interesting texture to
the meal.

The cold meat dishes are a joy to the active housewife
for they may be cooked ahead in the cool of the evening,
when the temperature drops, and chilled ready for serving
in the heat of the next day. Cold joints of meat make
ideal summer party fare.

Tasty cold meat loaf is another family favourite, easy
to make and easy to serve.

Meat has a natural delicious flavour of its own, but
this should be added to in hot climates, by cooking with
hot spices, vegetable flavourings and even wine, cider
or beer. Remember also when serving cold meat that when
food is chilled it sometimes tends to lose some flavour.
If possible, remove cold meat dishes from the refrigerator
$\frac{1}{2}$–1 hour before serving so that they can develop their
natural flavour again at room temperature. It is also
a good idea to serve hot fruit chutneys, pickles, relishes
and mustard with cold meat in hot weather, in order to
add 'pep' to the flavour.

Cold Loin of Pork Oriental

Barbecues are a popular way to feed family and friends.
A mid-day barbecue or an evening barbecue is always a
happy, relaxing affair. Food may be quite simple, chops,
sausages or steaks, or you may serve a more elaborate dish
such as kebabs.
Try the exciting barbecue recipes in this chapter for
Beef Sate or Barbecued Spiced Scallops. These
use spicy marinades which are easy to make in
advance and the food is therefore full of delicious flavour.
Serve with a refreshing salad and potato salad or rice
to complete the meal and make your barbecues a special
summer event.
Hot, spicy dishes, such as curries, are also excellent
hot weather food. Curries, like many cold meat dishes,
may be prepared in the cool of the evening and reheated
and served the next day. This gives the curry time to
mature in flavour. Hot spicy dishes cool the body and
they should be accompanied by hot lime or mango pickles
and chutneys, and refreshing sambals (side dishes) such as sliced
banana sprinkled with lime or lemon juice, or cool
cucumber, sliced thinly and mixed with natural yoghurt.
Take a lesson from other hot climate countries and add
spices to your main course, whether cold meat or a fish
dish or hot, spicy barbecues and curries. Accompany
them with cool and unusual side dishes and salads.
Jaded appetites will be stimulated and hot weather meals
will be a real pleasure.

Cold Loin of Pork Oriental

Serves 8–10

Time 2½–3 hours
Temperature 350–400°F.

1 × 5 lb loin of pork
dry mustard
4 fl oz sherry
4 fl oz soy sauce
1 tablespoon grated fresh ginger or 2 teaspoons ground ginger
2–4 cloves garlic, crushed
8 oz red currant jelly
extra 2 tablespoons sherry
extra 2 tablespoons soy sauce

Ask your butcher to bone and roll the loin of pork. Rub pork with mustard.
Prepare a marinade by mixing together the sherry, soy sauce, ginger and garlic. Pour marinade over pork and marinate for 2 hours, turning meat occasionally.
Place pork on a rack in a roasting pan and cook in a moderate oven for 2½–3 hours or until meat is cooked.
Baste pork with marinade while roasting.
Place red currant jelly in a saucepan and melt over a low heat. Stir in extra sherry and soy sauce and heat for 1 minute. Spoon jelly over loin of pork and stand in a cold place.
Serve cold roast pork at room temperature, if possible, accompanied with Green Salad (see page 62), Cabbage Salad (see page 59) and Potato Salad (see page 60).

31

Cold Baked Silverside of Beef

Serves 10–12

Time 3–4 hours
Temperature 325–350 °F.

5–6 lb. silverside of beef or top sirloin roast (salted)
2 carrots
2 onions
1 clove garlic, crushed
1 bay leaf
6 peppercorns
2 cloves
8 fl oz beer or red wine

Soak the beef in cold water for at least 2 hours before
baking it.
Place the beef in a large ovenproof casserole or pot-roaster.
Peel the carrots and onions, cut into chunky pieces and
add to the casserole. Add the crushed garlic, bay leaf,
peppercorns, cloves, beer or wine and sufficient cold water
to cover the beef.
Cover and cook in a moderately slow oven for 3–4 hours
or until tender. Test with a skewer or a fork, it should
come out easily if the meat is cooked.
Remove the beef and place in a large bowl. Put a plate
or a board on top and a heavy weight. Leave to stand
overnight if possible.
Serve beef cold with a fruit chutney, Tomato Salad (see page 60
and Green Salad (see page 84)
Note: The stock may be used to make a delicious chilled soup.

Cold Baked Silverside
of Beef with Green Salad

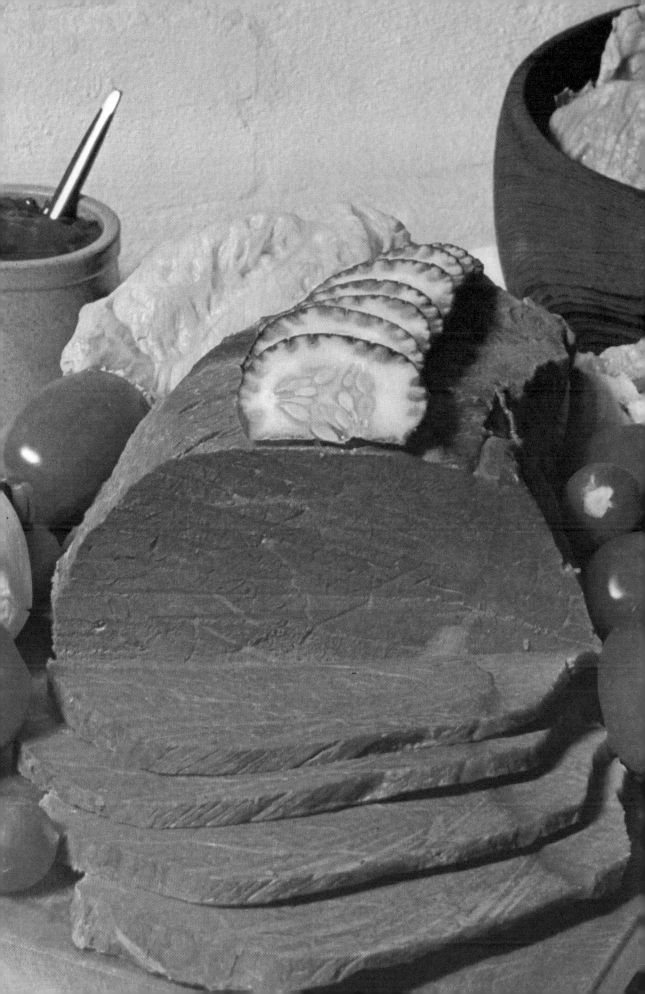

Cold Fillet of Beef

Serves 8–10

Time 45 minutes
Temperature 400–450°F.

1 × 3 lb fillet of beef
freshly ground black pepper
2 oz butter
2 tablespoons olive oil

Trim fillet of beef, removing all fat and tissue. Sprinkle
with freshly ground black pepper. Melt butter, mix with
olive oil and brush all over the beef. Wrap fillet of beef
in greased aluminium foil. Place on a rack in a roasting
pan and cook in a hot oven for 30 minutes. Unwrap foil
and allow beef to cook for a further 15 minutes or until
cooked as desired.
Transfer beef to a carving board and leave to cool.
Serve beef cold, carved in thin slices, and accompanied
with French mustard or Horseradish Cream (see recipe below)
and mixed salads.

Horseradish Cream

Makes approx. ¾ pint

12 fl oz fresh or sour cream
1 × 5 oz jar horseradish relish

If using fresh cream, whip until stiff and mix
with the horseradish relish.
If using sour cream, mix the two ingredients
together until evenly combined.
Chill Horseradish Cream before serving.
Delicious served with cold roast beef and cold
baked ham.

34

Mayonnaise

Makes approx. ½ pint

2 egg yolks
½ teaspoon salt
½ teaspoon sugar
½ teaspoon dry mustard
pinch of white pepper
1 teaspoon lemon juice
2½ pint olive oil
2–3 tablespoons white wine vinegar

Place the egg yolks in a mixing bowl, add seasonings
and lemon juice and mix until smooth, using a wooden
spoon or a sauce whisk.
Add 2 tablespoons oil, 2–3 drops at a time, stirring
continuously. Add 1 tablespoon vinegar and mix to the
consistency of cream.
Continue to add oil slowly, whisking continuously.
As the mayonnaise sauce thickens, add the oil more
quickly in a steady stream, whisking continuously. Add
a little vinegar from time to time to prevent
mayonnaise from becoming too thick.
When complete the mayonnaise should be stiff enough
to hold its shape.
Serve with fresh seafood or use to combine ingredients
in salads.

Dressed Crab

Serves 1

1 × 1–2 lb crab
salt and pepper
$\frac{1}{4}$ teaspoon dry mustard
1 hard-boiled egg
crisp lettuce leaves for garnish

If the crab is alive, boil it gently in salted water
for 15 minutes per pound. Cool crab in the liquid, then
take out and leave until quite cold.
To dress crab, first remove big claws and twist off the
small claws. Remove the crab's undershell.
Remove and discard the small sac from the top of the
crab's shell, any green matter and the spongy fingers
or lungs which lie around the big shell.
Scrape the brown creamy part of the crab into a bowl.
Remove the white flesh from the crab, separating it from
the inner shell with a skewer or a pointed vegetable knife.
Wash the shell well, using a small brush if necessary,
dry well.
Crack the big claws, remove all the meat and shred it using
a fork. Mix all the white meat together. Mix the brown
creamy part with salt, pepper and mustard. Place the brown
mixture across the centre of the shell with the white meat
on either side. Garnish with chopped egg white and sieved
egg yolk.
Serve dressed crab on a bed of lettuce leaves and accompany
with segments of lemon or mayonnaise.

Salmon Mousse

Serves 8–10

6 hard-boiled eggs
4 gherkins
1½ tablespoons gelatine
8 fl oz hot water
8 fl oz white wine
½ white vinegar
4 fl oz lemon juice
1 × 15 oz can salmon
salt and pepper
lettuce leaves and tomatoes for garnish

Rinse a mould with cold water and decorate with
slices of hard-boiled egg and gherkin. Dissolve
gelatine in hot water, and stir in wine, vinegar
and lemon juice. Pour a little gelatine mixture
over egg and gherkin decoration and refrigerate until set.
Drain salmon and flake well with a fork. Chop any
remaining hard-boiled egg and gherkin and mix with
the salmon. Add gelatine mixture and season to taste
with salt and pepper. Pour mixture into prepared
mould and refrigerate until set.
Turn out on to a flat serving plate and garnish with
small lettuce leaves and tomato wedges. Serve chilled
with Cucumber Sauce (see recipe opposite).

Cucumber Sauce

Makes approx. 1–1½ pints

2 small cucumbers
sugar
½ pint cream
4 tablespoons wine vinegar
salt
cayenne pepper

Peel cucumbers, remove seeds, and chop flesh into
fine dice. Sprinkle with sugar and leave to stand
for 1½–2 hours.
Whip cream until stiff, add well-drained cucumber,
vinegar and salt and cayenne pepper to taste. Mix
gently until ingredients are evenly combined.
Serve Cucumber Sauce immediately with Salmon Mousse
(see recipe opposite) or a fish salad.
Note: The sauce will become thin if left to stand
before serving.

Soused Fish

Serves 6

Time 3 hours
Temperature 300–325° F.

6 herring or mullet
1 onion, sliced
vinegar
water
4 bay leaves
2 cloves
12 allspice
2 blades of mace
1 teaspoon salt

Clean herrings and remove backbone. Lay herrings,
skin side down on working surface and place sliced
onion on centre of each fish. Roll fish up from
head to tail, secure with a toothpick.
Place fish in an ovenproof dish and add vinegar and
water to cover in the proportion of 3 parts vinegar to
1 part water. Add herbs, spices and salt.
Cover and cook in a slow oven for 3 hours, or until
fish is cooked. The liquid must not boil.
Transfer fish to a serving dish, strain liquor over,
cool then chill in refrigerator. The liquor sets in a
soft jelly.
Serve Soused Fish with Cucumber Salad (see page 66).

Soused Fish with Cucumber Salad

Seafood Salad

Serves 6–8

1 lettuce
8 oz prawns
8 oz crab
8 oz crayfish or lobster
8 oz white fish
4 tomatoes
8 olives
Dressing:
12 fl oz mayonnaise (see page 35)
juice of 1 lemon
1 tablespoon finely chopped onion
½ teaspoon dry mustard
pinch of saffron
salt and pepper

Line a salad bowl with crisp lettuce leaves. Prepare
prawns, crab and crayfish and steam white fish. Cut into
1 inch cubes and place attractively on top of lettuce.
Garnish with tomato wedges and olives.
Chill and serve with dressing.
Dressing: Mix mayonnaise with lemon juice, onion and
mustard. Dissolve saffron in a little hot water and stir
into the dressing. Add salt and pepper to taste. Chill
before serving.
Note: To steam fish, place skin side down on a plate
over a pan of gently boiling water. Season with pepper
and salt, add a little milk, cover with saucepan lid
and steam for 10–15 minutes or until fish is cooked.

Jellied Chicken

Serves 8–10

1 × 2½–3 lb chicken
1 onion
1 stalk celery
1 bay leaf
1 sprig parsley
salt
4 oz sliced ham
1 hard-boiled egg
1 gherkin
1 tablespoon gelatine
8 fl oz hot water
8 fl oz canned consommé
watercress sprigs for garnish

Wipe chicken with a clean, damp cloth. Peel onion
and cut celery into small pieces. Place onion, celery,
bay leaf and parsley into chicken's breast cavity. Sprinkle
chicken with salt, wrap securely in greased greaseproof
paper and steam for 1 hour or until tender. Cool.
Cut ham into neat circles, cut egg into circles and slice
gherkin into leaf shapes. Rinse a mould and decorate with
ham, egg and gherkin. Dissolve gelatine in hot water,
and mix with consommé. Pour a little jelly over decoration
and refrigerate until set. Remove flesh from chicken and
cut into ½ inch pieces. Chop scraps of remaining ham
finely. Mix chicken and ham with remaining gelatine
mixture, place gently over decoration in mould and chill
until set.
Unmould Jellied Chicken on to a serving plate, garnish
with watercress and serve with mixed salads or Cole Slaw
(see page 55).

Barbecued Beef Sate

Serves 6

2 lb rump steak
2 tablespoons soy sauce
1 tablespoon honey
2 cloves garlic, crushed
1 teaspoon ground coriander
1 teaspoon caraway seeds
$\frac{1}{4}$ teaspoon chilli powder
2 tablespoons vegetable oil

Cut steak into 1 inch cubes and place in a large bowl.
Mix remaining ingredients together and pour over
meat. Marinate for 1 hour, stirring occasionally.
Thread meat on to six skewers. Barbecue over hot
coals, turning occasionally, for 10 minutes or until
cooked to desired taste. Baste with marinade during
cooking.
Serve Beef Sate with Barbecue Sauce (see page 46) and
Green Salad (see page 62).

Barbecue Sauce

Makes $\frac{3}{4}$ pint

4 oz finely chopped onion
2 tablespoons brown sugar
2 tablespoons lime juice
1 tablespoon soy sauce
4 fl oz tomato sauce
4 fl oz water
freshly grown black pepper

Place all ingredients except pepper in a saucepan and heat gently, stirring continuously, until sugar is dissolved. Add pepper to taste.
Serve Barbecue Sauce with barbecued meat. Particularly delicious with Barbecued Beef Sate (see page 44).
Note: Lemon juice may be used in place of fresh lime juice.

Raisin Yellow Rice

Serves 6

$\frac{1}{2}$ oz butter
1 pint 4 fl oz chicken stock or 1 pint 4 fl oz water and
   3 chicken stock cubes
9 oz cups long grain rice
2 tablespoons sugar
1 teaspoon turmeric
3 oz seedless raisins
salt and pepper

Melt butter in a saucepan, add chicken stock and bring to the boil. Add rice and stir well. Turn down heat. Add remaining ingredients, with salt and pepper to taste and simmer, covered, for 20 minutes, or until liquid has been absorbed and grains are tender.
Serve hot with barbecued meat.

Barbecued Spiced Scallops

Serves 6

2 lb scallops
1 clove garlic, crushed
1 teaspoon grated root ginger
1 tablespoon sugar
4 fl soy sauce
4 fl oz dry sherry or sake
1 green pepper
4 oz small mushrooms

Place scallops in a bowl and add the next 5 ingredients.
Leave to marinate for 2 hours, at room temperature, stirring
occasionally.
Cut pepper in half, remove seeds and cut pepper into 1 inch
pieces. Wipe mushrooms with a clean, damp cloth.
Drain scallops and thread on to six skewers, alternating
with green pepper and mushrooms.
Barbecue over hot coals, turning occasionally, for 10–15
minutes or until cooked to taste. Baste with the marinade
before and during cooking.
Serve barbecued scallops hot with Cabbage Salad (see page 59)
or Cucumber Salad (see page 66).

Beef Curry

Serves 4

1 lb beef topside steak
1 tablespoon ground coriander
1 teaspoon ground turmeric
½ teaspoon cumin
¼ teaspoon chilli powder
pinch of ground cinnamon
2 cloves
1 bay leaf
3 tablespoons vinegar
2 tablespoons vegetable oil
1 onion, chopped
1 clove garlic, crushed
1 teaspoon salt
6 fl oz water and 1 beef stock cube

Cut beef into 1 inch cubes.
Mix and pound the spices with the vinegar to form a paste.
Heat oil in a heavy saucepan and fry onion and garlic
gently for 5 minutes. Add curry paste and fry for
2–3 minutes, stirring continuously. Add beef and cook
gently, stirring occasionally, until beef changes
colour. Add salt, water and beef stock cube, cover and
simmer for 1 hour.
Taste curry before serving and adjust flavour if
necessary.
Serve curry with boiled rice and sambals or side dishes such
as lime chutney, mango pickle, sliced banana, tomatoes in
lemon juice, sliced cucumber in yoghurt.

Beef Curry with side dishes

Glazed Baked Bacon

Serves 10–12

Time 2 hours
Temperature 375–400°F.

1 joint of bacon weighing 4–4½ lb
cloves
1 onion
1 carrot
2 stalks celery
1 pint cider or beer
2 tablespoons brown sugar
1 × 15 oz can apricot halves
10–12 maraschino or glacé cherries
sprigs of parsley or watercress for garnish

Soak the bacon in cold water for 6 hours if smoked,
for 2 hours if unsmoked. Drain well and remove the
rind. Place bacon on a rack in a roasting pan and
stud the fat side with cloves. Cut vegetables into
chunky pieces and add to bacon in roasting pan. Pour
cider over and sprinkle sugar over bacon joint.
Cover roasting pan with aluminium foil and cook in a
moderately hot oven for 1½ hours. Remove foil and place
drained apricot halves and cherries attractively on top
of bacon, securing with toothpicks. Baste well and cook,
uncovered for a further 20–30 minutes, basting occasionally.
Place bacon on a carving board. Allow to cool.
Garnish bacon with sprigs of parsley or watercress and
serve cold with a fruit chutney, Potato Salad (see page 60) and
Green Salad (see page 62).

Peach Chutney

Makes 3 pints

16 medium size peaches
6 oz raisins
8 oz brown sugar, firmly packed
6 fl oz cider vinegar
1 teaspoon cinnamon
½ tespoon ground cloves
2 teaspoons mustard seed
2 oz chopped nuts, optional

Peel peaches, remove stones and slice the fruit. Measure
8 cups of fruit and place in a large heavy-based pan. Add
remaining ingredients, except nuts. Bring to the boil and
simmer, uncovered, stirring frequently, for 45 minutes
or until mixture has thickened. Add nuts, if desired, and
cook a further 2 minutes.
Pour chutney into 6 sterilized ½ pint jars to within ½ inch
of the top and seal. Store in refrigerator and use within
2–3 weeks.
Serve chutney with slices of cold meat and salad.
Variation: Try making this chutney with apricots,
nectarines or mangoes.

Salads

When summer comes we always think of salads and slimming! Salads should be imaginative, crisp, refreshing and delicious.

There are always interesting, colourful salad vegetables in season to make tasty, attractive salads. Add variety of flavour and texture to these with the addition of fruit, nuts or fresh herbs. Citrus fruit is particularly refreshing in mixed salads as it contains a lot of juice. Use segments of grapefruit, slices of orange or lemon or lime juice in your salads. Pineapple is another refreshing salad ingredient.

Meat, fish or eggs may be added to mixed salads to make a substantial, balanced meal. Toss salads in cool dressings made from mayonnaise, sour cream, yoghurt or an acidic French dressing.

Salad plants must always be fresh and crisp and require careful preparation. Ideally, salad greens should be used straight from the garden, but if this is not possible, they should be washed and dried carefully and then crisped up in the refrigerator before serving. Simple green salads should be tossed in dressing at the last minute, just before serving, otherwise they will lose their crispness. This kind of salad, tossed in French dressing, makes an excellent accompaniment in hot weather for barbecued fish or meat or quickly grilled meat.

Two salad 'standbys' are the traditional French dressing and mayonnaise dressing. French dressing is made from three parts of olive oil to one part of vinegar. The vinegar should be a good quality wine vinegar or herb-flavoured vinegar. Add salt and freshly-ground pepper to taste. A good pinch of sugar and dry mustard add flavour. A clove of crushed garlic

Cole Slaw ingredients

is another traditional flavouring. Various herbs may
be chopped and added to the dressing to enhance its
flavour; parsley, chives, mint, dill and tarragon
are among the most popular used.
Mayonnaise, another classical dressing, is popular
mixed with salads. It is often served separately in
a sauceboat. However, for refreshingly different
salad dressings in a hot climate, try natural yoghurt,
sour cream, lime juice or lemon juice.
The attraction of a salad depends greatly on its
appearance. It should look light and delicate and
be fresh and neat in presentation. Be adventurous
with your salad creations. Try serving Cole Slaw
with cold pork, Cucumber Salad with cold fish mousse,
Carrot Salad with barbecued meat.
Remember always to prepare the salad ingredients
carefully, taste the dressing and adjust the flavour,
and serve the salad crisp and chilled.

Carrot Salad

Serves 6–8

2 oz soft breadcrumbs
1 oz butter
2 oz peanuts, shelled
6 medium carrots, grated
2 tablespoons vegetable oil
1 tablespoon white vinegar
salt and pepper

Fry breadcrumbs in the butter until crisp and
golden. Add peanuts and mix well. Cool. Add grated
carrot, oil, vinegar and salt and pepper to taste. Toss
lightly.
Chill before serving.

Cole Slaw

Serves 12

1 small firm cabbage
3 red apples
6 oz raisins
Dressing:
6 tablespoons olive oil
1 tablespoon lemon juice
1 tablespoon orange juice
1 tablespoon Worcestershire sauce
2 tablespoons finely chopped onion
1 tablespoon chopped stuffed olives
1 tablespoon chopped parsley
$\frac{1}{2}$ teaspoon dry mustard
$\frac{1}{2}$ teaspoon salt
$\frac{1}{4}$ teaspoon pepper

Shred cabbage finely, removing any coarse stem.
Remove cores from apples, do not peel. Dice apples
and add to cabbage. Add raisins, which have been
previously soaked in $\frac{1}{2}$ cup hot water for 5–10
minutes. Add dressing and toss until salad is evenly
coated.
Serve chilled with cold ham or cold pork.
Dressing: Mix all ingredients together.

Greek Salata

Serves 10–12

½ small red cabbage, shredded
4 oz cooked beetroot cut in julienne strips
4 oz cooked green beans
1 tablespoon capers
1 tablespoon chopped olives
1 quantity French dressing (see page 63)

Place prepared cabbage, beetroot and beans in a salad bowl. Sprinkle capers and olives over salad.
Pour dressing over salad and chill for at least 30 minutes.
Serve salad chilled with cold meat or barbecued meat.

Green Bean Salad

Serves 6–8

1½ lb green beans
2 large tomatoes, peeled and chopped
1 onion, sliced
1 teaspoon sugar
½ teaspoon dried oregano
½ teaspoon salt
freshly ground black pepper
2 fl oz olive oil

Top and tail and string beans. Place in a pan of boiling, salted water and boil for 5 minutes. Drain, cool and chill.
Gently mix beans with remaining ingredients and chill.
Serve with cold meat or fish salads.

Cool Radish Salad

Serves 6–8

1 bunch radishes
1 small cucumber
½ pint sour cream
juice of 1 lemon
salt and pepper
extra radishes and parsley sprigs for garnish

Slice radishes into fine circles. Peel cucumber and
slice finely. Mix radishes and cucumber with sour
cream, lemon juice and salt and pepper to taste. Place
in a salad bowl and chill for at least 1 hour.
Garnish salad with extra radishes and parsley and serve
chilled with cold beef or cold meat loaf.

Mushroom Bean Salad

Serves 4–6

1 × 10 oz can lima or broad beans
6 oz mushrooms, sliced
1 teaspoon finely chopped onion
½ teaspoon ground nutmeg
1 quantity French dressing (see page 63)

Drain beans into a strainer and rinse under cold
running water. Drain well.
Mix beans with sliced raw mushrooms, onion and nutmeg.
Pour French dressing over and chill for at least 1 hour.
Serve salad with cold meat or barbecued meat.

Pea Salad

Serves 4–6

1 × 12 oz packet frozen peas
4 oz mushrooms, thinly sliced
2 stalks celery, finely sliced
2 tablespoons sultanas, optional
2 tablespoons olive oil
2 tablespoons wine vinegar
salt and pepper
¼ teaspoon dry mustard
1 teaspoon sugar
1 clove garlic, crushed

Cook the peas according to the directions on the packet.
Drain and cool.
Mix the cold peas with the sliced raw mushrooms and celery
in a salad bowl. Add sultanas if desired.
Place remaining ingredients in a screw-top jar, cover
and shake well. Pour dressing over pea mixture and chill well.

Cabbage Salad

Serves 6–8

the heart of 1 small red cabbage or ½ red cabbage
salt
3 tablespoons olive oil
2 tablespoons white wine vinegar
1 teaspoon sugar
freshly ground pepper
1 onion, finely chopped
2 red eating apples, cored and sliced or diced

Shred cabbage finely, sprinkle with salt and allow
to stand for 1 hour. Press cabbage well to drain
off liquor.
Make dressing by mixing together olive oil, vinegar,
sugar, salt and pepper in a screw-top jar.
Pour dressing over cabbage. Add onion and apple.

Tomato Salad

Serves 4–6

1 lb tomatoes
1 tablespoon chopped fresh basil
   or 1 teaspoon dried basil
finely grated rind of 1 lemon
1 quantity French dressing (see page 63)

Slice tomatoes thinly and place in a flat shallow
dish. Sprinkle tomatoes with basil, lemon rind and
French dressing. Chill for 30 minutes.
Serve Tomato Salad with cold meat, cold fish salads
or barbecued meat.
Variation: Add 2 oranges, peeled and segmented neatly,
for a refreshing salad.

Potato Salad

Serves 4–6

1 lb potatoes
1 small onion, finely chopped
1 Granny Smith apple, peeled and chopped
1 dill pickle, chopped
$\frac{1}{2}$ pint sour cream
juice of 1 lemon
salt and pepper

Boil potatoes in skins. Drain and cool. Peel
potatoes thinly and cut into $\frac{1}{2}$–1 inch cubes. Add
chopped onion, apple and dill pickle. Add sour cream
and lemon juice and mix gently until potatoes are well
coated. Season to taste with salt and pepper.
Serve chilled in a chilled salad bowl.
Note: Any sweet, crisp apple can be used. The
Granny Smith has a green skin.

                                  Tomato Salad with orange segments

Green Salad

Serves 6–8

1 lettuce
½ cucumber
1 green pepper
parsley sprigs, optional
watercress sprigs, optional
1 quantity French dressing (see recipe opposite).

Prepare lettuce. Firstly remove outside leaves which
are dirty, bruised or limp. Remove core of lettuce with
a sharp vegetable knife. Hold lettuce upside down under
a cold flowing tap, allowing water to run into centre
of lettuce. Turn lettuce over and allow to drain. Gently
peel lettuce leaves apart, place in a clean tea towel,
roll up gently and shake well to remove water. Place
lettuce in a plastic container in refrigerator and chill
until crisp.
Peel cucumber and cut into thin slices.
Wash and seed green pepper and cut into thin rings.
Place crisp lettuce, torn into bite-sized pieces, into
a chilled salad bowl. Add prepared cucumber, green pepper
and parsley and watercress sprigs if desired. Pour
French dressing over and gently roll the salad in this
with clean hands until each leaf is glistening with
dressing.
Serve immediately with cold meat or barbecued meat.

French Dressing

3 tablespoons olive oil
1 tablespoon herb flavoured or wine vinegar
1 teaspoon sugar
½ teaspoon dry mustard
½ teaspoon salt
freshly ground black pepper
1 clove garlic, crushed
1 tablespoon chopped fresh herbs, optional

Place all ingredients in a screw-top jar and shake
well until evenly mixed.
Alternatively all the dry ingredients may be placed
in a salad bowl and the liquid ingredients added
slowly, whisking continuously until smoothly combined.
Use to dress salads and to dress hors d'oeuvre dishes.
Note: Larger quantities of French Dressing may be
prepared and stored in a screw-top jar in the refrigerator
for a few weeks.
A good quality salad oil may be used instead of olive
oil and white vinegar may be used instead of herb flavoured
or wine vinegar. However, for a good flavoured dressing,
try the given recipe.

Citrus Green Salad

Serves 6–8

1 lettuce
1 bunch watercress
2 grapefruit
2 oranges
1 quantity French dressing (see page 63)

Prepare lettuce (see Green Salad, page 62) and crispen
in refrigerator.
Wash watercress sprigs and dry in a clean tea towel.
Crispen in refrigerator.
Remove peel carefully from grapefruit and oranges, using
a sharp, serrated knife. Make sure all pith is removed.
Cut grapefruit and oranges into sections and place in
a chilled salad bowl.
Add lettuce, torn into bite-sized pieces, and watercress
sprigs. Pour French dressing over and toss salad gently
with clean hands until each leaf is coated with dressing.
Serve salad immediately. Delicious served with rye bread
and cheese for a quick summer lunch.

Cucumber Salad

Serves 6

2 medium size cucumbers
1 teaspoon salt
1 small onion, finely chopped
3 tablespoons white vinegar
1 tablespoon water
1 teaspoon sugar
$\frac{1}{4}$ teaspoon white pepper

Wash and dry cucumbers and score the skin lengthways
with the prongs of a fork. Slice cucumbers very thinly.
Sprinkle with salt and leave to stand for 1 hour.
Drain off liquid, pressing cucumbers to drain as much
as possible.
Mix remaining ingredients together with salt and pepper
to taste and pour over cucumbers. Chill. Drain off
liquor just before serving.
Serve with cold fish or meat, barbecued meat and
curries.

Avocado Fancy Salad Bowl

Serves 6–8

1 lettuce
1 × 16 oz can asparagus spears
1 × 14 oz can artichoke hearts
1 avocado pear
1 tablespoon pitted, sliced olives
1 quantity French dressing (see page 63)

Wash lettuce, dry well in a clean tea towel, refrigerate
in an air-tight container to crispen.
Drain asparagus and artichokes. Peel avocado pear, remove
seed and cut avocado into slices.
Tear lettuce in bite-sized pieces into a chilled salad
bowl. Add asparagus, artichokes and olives. Add French
dressing and toss gently until all lettuce leaves glisten
with dressing. Arrange avocado slices attractively on
top of salad.
Serve salad immediately. Delicious with Cold
Fillet of Beef (see page 34).

Beetroot Salad

Serves 8–10

1 tablespoon gelatine
3 tablespoons hot water
16 fl oz boiling water
3 tablespoons wine vinegar
12 oz chopped cooked beetroot
1 stalk celery, chopped, optional
1 teaspoon horseradish relish
salt and pepper

Dissolve gelatine in 3 tablespoons hot water. Add
boiling water and vinegar. Allow to cool.
Stir in chopped beetroot, celery if desired and horseradish
relish. Season to taste with salt and pepper.
Pour mixture into a previously rinsed mould or a serving
dish and chill in refrigerator until set.
Serve Beetroot Salad with cold beef or ham.

The Dessert Course

Fresh fruit desserts are ideal for hot climates.
They are refreshing and full of delicious, natural
juicy flavours.
Cold sweets using fresh fruit are simple to make and
there are many to choose from. Try the recipes given
in this chapter. Most of them require no cooking at
all so you can keep your kitchen cool. Others require
slight cooking to thicken custards and dissolve gelatine
for soufflés and mousses. All the desserts should be
chilled in the refrigerator before serving.
The most popular hot weather desserts are ice cream,
fruit salad, fruit creams, fruit mousses, soufflés
and jellies.
Fresh fruits form the basis of many of these recipes,
but if they are not available, canned, bottled, frozen
and even dried fruit may be used as an alternative.
Cream may be substituted with evaporated milk. This
has a more definite flavour which may be overcome by
the addition of a little lemon juice.
Try to make your own ice cream. I have given you two
recipes for this. One is suitable for everyday meals,
the other is much richer and is deliciously creamy, so
serve it to impress your friends on special occasions.
Colour and flavour balance is important when making
desserts. Tropical fruits have beautiful colours,
ranging from the pale gold of lime juice and bananas,
to the rich orange of mangoes and pawpaws.
These colours and flavours blend perfectly with berry
fruits such as strawberries and raspberries, with
delicious stone fruits such as peaches, nectarines and
apricots, and also with the fruits of the vine—grapes
and passionfruit.

Brandied Strawberries

Chilled fresh fruit or fruit salad is always an easy
dessert to serve in hot weather, but do try to give
it a little variety. Fruit creams, mousses
and soufflés are quite easy to make if you follow
the recipes carefully. They also look attractive and
have a rich, creamy, melt-in-the-mouth texture. They
may be made in advance so they are ideal to serve at
a dinner party.
Cool desserts need not be elaborate, but they should
be attractive and tempting to look at, as well as
delicious to eat. Serve them in simple dishes—
in well polished glass bowls or glazed china, or in
individual glasses which can be chilled in the
refrigerator—and you will serve them with pride.

Melon Fruit Cup

Serves 4–6

2 oranges
seedless grapes
1 small melon, diced
juice of 1 lemon
2 tablespoons sugar
fresh mint leaves for decoration, optional

Peel and section oranges, using a sharp serrated
knife. Place oranges in a bowl and add grapes, melon,
lemon juice and sugar. Mix lightly and chill.
Serve chilled, decorated with fresh mint if desired.

Brandied Strawberries

Serves 6

3 large punnets strawberries
2 tablespoons icing sugar
6 tablespoons brandy or grand marnier

Place fresh strawberries in a bowl and sprinkle
with icing sugar and brandy. Leave to stand at
room temperature for at least 1 hour.
Serve in individual glasses, accompanied with thin
pouring cream if desired.

Ice Cream

Serves 12

1 × 20 oz can evaporated milk
1 teaspoon gelatine
1 tablespoon hot water
1 tablespoon sugar
2 tablespoons sherry
lemon or pink colouring, optional

Chill evaporated milk in refrigerator, overnight if
possible.
Dissolve gelatine in hot water. Whip evaporated milk
in a chilled mixing bowl until stiff. Stir in sugar, sherry
and cool dissolved gelatine. Add colouring to make a
pastel shade, if desired. Beat mixture for a further
minute and pour into two refrigerator trays. Place in
freezer to set.
Serve Ice Cream with fruit salad.
Variation: To make Cassata, add $\frac{1}{4}$ cup chopped cherries,
$\frac{1}{4}$ cup chopped almonds or walnuts and $\frac{1}{2}$ cup raisins to
mixture before freezing.

Fruits in Syrup

Serves 6–8

2 tablespoons sugar
4 tablespoons water
2 tablespoons dry sherry
2 teaspoons lemon or lime juice
½ teaspoon cinnamon
1 orange
1 medium pineapple, cubed
6 oz fresh mango or pawpaw cubes
9 oz lychees

Dissolve sugar in water in a saucepan. Cool.
Stir in sherry, lemon juice and cinnamon.
Peel and segment orange neatly. Mix with remaining
fruit. Pour syrup over and chill for 1 hour.
Serve from chilled fruit bowl.
Note: If mango and pawpaw are unobtainable,
peaches or apricots may be substituted.

Melon Ambrosia

Serves 10–12

12 oz rock melon or canteloup balls or diced melon
12 oz honeydew melon balls or diced melon
2 oranges, peeled and sectioned
2 bananas, sliced
6 oz strawberries
3 oz green grapes
3 oz black or purple grapes
6 oz diced pawpaw or peach
4 tablespoons sugar
juice of 1 lemon
1 oz shredded coconut

Prepare fruit, mix with sugar and lemon juice and
chill. Serve topped with a sprinkling of coconut.
Note: Any colourful mixture of fruit may be added to the melon.

Banana Rum Mousse

Serves 6–8

1 packet lemon jelly (lemon jello)
2 large bananas, mashed
8 fl oz cream
2 tablespoons rum
extra whipped cream for serving

Make lemon jelly and chill until half set. Add mashed
bananas, whipped cream and rum and beat until smooth.
Pour into a serving dish and refrigerate until set.
Serve chilled, topped with whipped cream.

Banana Ice Cream

Serves 6–8

4 large bananas, mashed
1½ cups sugar
pinch of salt
4 fl oz pineapple juice
juice of 1 lemon
2 tablespoons rum
1 teaspoon powdered ginger
½ pint cream

Mix together all ingredients, except cream, until
evenly combined. Whip cream and fold into mixture.
Place mixture in a refrigerator tray and place in
freezer until edges are mushy. Turn out into a
mixing bowl and beat until frothy. Return to refrigerator
tray and freeze until set.
Serve in chilled glasses.

Lemon Cream Soufflé

Serves 6–8

3 eggs
6 oz castor sugar or powdered sugar
juice of 3 lemons
1 tablespoon gelatine
3 tablespoons hot water
½ pint cream or chilled evaporated milk
2 tablespoons chopped nuts, 4 fl oz extra cream
and 2 passionfruit or sliced fresh peach or segmented
mandarin for decoration

Secure a double piece of greaseproof paper or aluminium
foil around edge of a 2 pint soufflé dish, to come 3–4
inches above top of dish.
Place egg yolks, sugar and lemon juice in the top of
a double boiler, or in a heatproof bowl placed over a
saucepan of gently boiling water, and beat until mixture
thickens. Remove from heat, continue beating until
lukewarm.
Dissolve gelatine in 3 tablespoons hot water, stand aside
until lukewarm, then stir quickly in a thin continuous
stream into the egg yolk mixture. Both mixtures should
be at body temperature to combine correctly.
Whip cream until thick. Whisk egg white until stiff.
Fold cream and egg whites evenly into egg/lemon mixture,
pour into prepared soufflé dish and refrigerate until
set.
When set, remove band of paper and spoon chopped nuts
on to sides of soufflé. Decorate top edge with rosettes
of whipped cream and put passionfruit, peach or mandarin segments
in centre on top of soufflé.
Serve soufflé the same day it is made for best flavour
and texture.

Oranges and Grapes Grand Marnier

Serves 6

6 oranges
8 oz grapes
8 oz castor sugar or powdered sugar
4 fl oz water
juice of 1 lemon
6 tablespoons grand marnier
6 oz slivered almonds

Peel oranges with a sharp serrated knife. Take care
to remove all the rind and pith. Slice oranges across
thinly and place in a large bowl.
Wash, halve and deseed the grapes and add to sliced
oranges.
Place sugar and water in a saucepan and put over a
low heat. Stir until sugar is dissolved and bring
to the boil. Simmer for 1 minute, remove from heat,
add lemon juice and grand marnier.
Arrange oranges and grapes attractively in a serving
dish. Pour syrup over. Sprinkle with slivered almonds.
Chill well.
Serve with cream if desired.

Grapefruit Mousse

Serves 6

2 eggs
4 oz castor sugar or powdered sugar
1 large grapefruit
1 tablespoon gelatine
3 tablespoons hot water
$\frac{1}{2}$ pint cream
grapefruit segments for decoration

Separate eggs. Place egg yolks with castor sugar,
finely grated grapefruit rind and strained grapefruit
juice in the top of a double boiler. Beat over gently
bubbling water until mixture thickens. Cool.
Dissolve gelatine in hot water. Cool. Pour gelatine
into egg yolk mixture, in a steady stream, stirring
continuously. Both mixtures should be at body temperature
to combine correctly.
Whip cream until thick and whisk egg whites until stiff.
Fold into the egg/grapefruit mixture. Pour into a glass
serving bowl and refrigerate until set.
Serve chilled, decorated with grapefruit segments.

78

Quick Orange Jelly/Jello

Serves 4–6

1 tablespoon gelatine
4 fl oz hot water
½ pint canned or fresh orange juice, chilled
6 crushed ice cubes

Dissolve gelatine in hot water.
Add chilled orange juice and stir in crushed
ice until ice melts.
Pour into a jelly mould, previously rinsed with
cold water, and refrigerate until set.
Serve jelly chilled with a fruit salad, cream or
ice cream, if desired.

Orange Creams

Serves 4

1 tablespoon gelatine
3 tablespoons hot water
16 fl oz canned or fresh orange juice, chilled
4 fl oz cream, whipped

Dissolve gelatine in hot water.
Add chilled orange juice and stir thoroughly.
Stir in whipped cream and pour into 4 individual
moulds, previously rinsed with cold water.
Stand moulds on ice tray and surround with ice.
Place in a freezer for 10–15 minutes or until
set.
Turn out and serve immediately or transfer to
food compartment of refrigerator until ready to
serve.

79

Italian Lemon Water Ice

Serves 6

$\frac{1}{2}$ pint lemon juice (approx. 6 lemons)
8 oz sugar
1 pint water
1 egg white, optional

Thinly pare the rind from 2 lemons. Squeeze the
juice from all the lemons.
Place sugar and water in a saucepan and heat gently
until sugar dissolves. Add lemon rind and boil gently
for 10 minutes. Leave to cool. Add the lemon juice
and strain into an ice-cube tray.
Place in the freezing compartment of the refrigerator
and leave until half frozen, about 1 hour. Turn mixture
into a bowl and fold in stiffly whisked egg white, if
desired. Return to ice-cube tray and re-freeze.
Serve in glasses or in the empty lemon caps. Cut a
slice from the bottom of each lemon cap before filling
with water ice, so that it will stand firmly.

Italian Lemon Water Ice (front)

Pineapple in Sour Cream

Serves 6

3 teaspoons gelatine
2 fl oz hot water
8 fl oz pineapple juice
6 oz chopped pineapple
8 fl oz sour cream
whipped cream for serving

Dissolve gelatine in hot water.
Add pineapple juice and chill in refrigerator until
beginning to set.
Fold in chopped pineapple and sour cream.
Put mixture into 6 individual glasses and chill well
until set.
Serve topped with whipped cream.

82

Iced Cream Cheese

Serves 6

8 oz cream cheese
8 fl oz cream
finely grated rind of 1 lemon
castor sugar or powdered sugar

Sieve cream cheese. Whip cream and mix with sieved
cheese until smooth. Add lemon rind and castor sugar
to taste.
Press mixture into a round container, previously lined
with muslin. Cover with aluminium foil and place in
freezer for 1–2 hours.
Turn out and serve with fresh berry fruit such as
strawberries, raspberries or red or black currants.

Cool Drinks

Sipping Cool Drinks is a pleasurably soothing hot
weather pastime. Cool Drinks are also good for you
because they quench the thirst and replace important
moisture lost in a hot climate.

I have given you some recipes for the ever popular
milkshake for children, refreshing iced coffee and
tea for adults, and long Cool Drinks and punches,
some alcoholic, some non-alcoholic.

Cool Drinks are instant refreshers in hot weather.
They are sure of a welcome at any summer party, for
they are good companions to cool food, refreshing
salads and spicy barbecues.

Fresh, citrus fruit drinks, with their sharp, tangy
flavour, are probably one of the most popular summer
thirst quenchers.

Cool alcoholic drinks are hot climate vitalizers.
Served chilled before a meal, they relax the mind
and stimulate the appetite; the meal to follow is
much more enjoyable.

Long Cool Drinks deserve tall, chilled, attractive
glasses. Chill the glasses in a refrigerator if
possible or with a special glass frosting gadget. If
the glasses are not chilled, add plenty of ice before
pouring in the drink, in order to serve it cold.

Colourful garnishes of sliced citrus fruit, oranges,
lemons and limes, cherries and strawberries and strips
of cucumber add a touch of sophistication to cool
drinks. They also give the party look that children
enjoy. So be a success this summer and serve Cool
Drinks with the professional touch.

Champagne and Orange Juice

Champagne and Orange Juice

For a festive occasion add chilled strained
fresh orange juice to equal quantities of
iced champagne.
Serve immediately.

Iced Orange

Serves 10

maraschino cherries
1 orange, sliced
½ bottle orange cordial
1 pint 4 fl oz iced water
2 small bottles ginger ale

Make ice cubes with a cherry in the centre of each.
Place orange slices in a large chilled jug. Add
orange cordial, iced water and ginger ale.
Serve chilled with ice cubes in each glass.

Orange Milk Shake

Serves 4

juice of 3 oranges
juice of 1 grapefruit
2 tablespoons sugar
1 pint chilled milk

Mix all ingredients together in a blender.
Pour into tall glasses and serve immediately.

Wine Cooler

Serves 24

12 oz berry fruit, raspberries or cranberries
3 bananas, diced
1 medium pineapple, chopped or 1 × 15 oz can
    pineapple pieces with juice
1 × 26 fl oz bottle lemonade
1 × 26 fl oz bottle rosé wine
1 × 26 fl oz bottle dry or sweet white wine

Mix berry fruit with bananas, pineapple and lemonade.
Chill well, overnight if possible.
Place ¼ cup fruit mixture in each tall glass. Add
ice cubes and fill glass with either rosé or white
wine.
Serve immediately with a tall spoon.

Sherry Refresher

Serves 4–6

juice of 3 grapefruit
4 fl oz dry or sweet sherry
soda water

Strain grapefruit juice into a jug.
Add sherry and chill well in refrigerator.
Serve chilled, 'topped up' with soda water to taste.

Iced Tea

Make a strong 'brew' of tea, cool and chill well.
Pour chilled tea into tall glasses over ice cubes
and serve with lemon wedges. Add a pinch of cinnamon
or mixed spice to each glass. Add sugar if desired.

Berry Milk Shake

Serves 6–8

1 large brick ice cream
1 × 10 oz can raspberries
1 pint 12 fl oz milk

Place all ingredients together in a blender and
mix until smoothly combined.
Serve in chilled glasses.

Cider Cup

Serves 10–12

1 teacup mint leaves
2 × 26 fl oz bottles of cider
16 fl oz pineapple juice
2 large bottles ginger ale

Crush mint leaves and place in a large jug. Add cider
and pineapple juice. Chill well.
Serve chilled, 'topped up' with ginger ale.

Iced Coffee

Make some strong coffee using $1\frac{1}{2}$ teaspoons instant
coffee or 1 tablespoon ground coffee per person.
Cool and chill well.
Pour chilled coffee into tall glasses over ice cubes.
Serve topped with lighly whipped cream and grated chocolate.
Add sugar if desired.

Glossary

A glossary of terms used
in this book:

allspice
a mildly sharp and fragrant spice;
also known as pimento.

basil
an aromatic herb used in salads,
soups, stews and sauces;
excellent with tomato salads.

baste
to spoon liquid over food as
it cooks.

blanch
to pre-heat in boiling water
in order to whiten meats,
or to loosen skins of nuts or fruits.

bouillon
a clear soup, usually made
from beef.

bouillon cube
a soup or stock cube used to
flavour soups and stews.

capers
the flower buds of a
Mediterranean shrub; pickled,
they are used for garnishing and
flavouring.

caraway
aromatic seedlike fruit of a herb.

cayenne (red) pepper
the most pungent of spices,
hot and biting; can vary from hot
to extremely hot depending on
the blend used.

cinnamon
a powder made from the sweet,
spicy bark of the cinnamon tree.

cloves
a hot sweet spice with a highly
aromatic scent; may be used
whole or ground for pickling,
glazing ham and in some desserts.

consommé
a clear soup which has a light
gelatinous texture when cool.

coriander
a spice used in the making of
curry paste.

cream cottage cheese
a cottage cheese made from cream
rather than skim or whole milk.

cumin
a spice which is also an ingredient
of curry powder and curry paste.

filleting knife
a small, sharp, pointed,
steel knife, used to fillet fish,
meat and poultry; a smaller
version of the French kitchen knife.

garlic
a pungent bulb; used crushed or
finely chopped, to flavour meats
and salads.

gherkin
the young fruit of the cucumber;
pickled, it is used for garnishing
and for flavouring salads
and cold meats.

grand marnier
an orange-flavoured, brandy-
based liqueur.

honeydew melon
a sweet-flavoured, white-fleshed
melon with a smooth, pale
green rind.

hors d'oeuvre
may be made up from meat,
fish, eggs, vegetables, salad or
fruit and from one or more
dishes; this term refers to the
appetizers served with cocktails
before sitting at the table;
hors d'oeuvre often form the
first course of the meal.

julienne
cut into fine strips about the size
of a matchstick.

ketchup
a thick, spicy, fruit sauce,
usually tomato-based; known as
'catsup' in some countries.

lychees
a small, soft, sweet, spicy fruit
with a fragile shell; available
in cans.

mace
the dried outer skin of the kernel
of the nutmeg; used in pickling
and in sweets and desserts.

maraschino cherries
cherries which are preserved and
bottled in maraschino; used to
decorate sweet dishes and
cool drinks.

marinade
a mixture of oil and an acid
such as vinegar, lemon juice
or wine, with the addition of
seasoning and flavourings;
used to 'marinate' or stand food in
for some time to give it more
flavour and to soften the tissues
of tough meat.

monosodium glutamate
a crystalline chemical product
added to food to bring out its
natural flavour; sometimes
called M.S.G. or accent.

oregano
a herb that is particularly good
with tomatoes and tomato sauces.

Parmesan
a hard, dry, strongly-flavoured
Italian cheese; usually finely
ground for cooking.

pawpaw or papaw
a fruit with rich orange flesh
grown in temperate and tropical
climates.

pot roaster
a flameproof, ovenproof casserole,
with a tight-fitting lid, in which
large joints of meat may be cooked
in the oven or on a hot plate.

port
a very sweet fortified red wine;
used to flavour desserts or as an
after dinner liqueur.

rock melon
a sweet-flavoured light orange
melon with a rough brownish
skin; often known as cantaloup.

saffron
a spice made from the stamens of
the violet-coloured crocus,
used to colour food bright orange.

sake
a Japanese alcoholic drink
made from rice.

sambals
accompaniments which are
served with curry; these may be
hot, fruit chutneys or cool fruits
and vegetables dressed in French
dressing, lemon juice or yoghurt.

sauté
to fry lightly in a small amount of
fat or oil, turning frequently
during cooking.

scallops
a mollusc with a rounded
fluted-edged shell; used in
seafood dishes.

sesame seeds
seeds of a tropical herbaceous
plant; the small oval seeds have a
delicious flavour and can be
ground to obtain an oil.

shallots
long thin young onions, called
spring onions in some countries;
these are known as scallions in
US.

shred
to slice into thin strips.

sosatie
a Cape Malay (South African)
dish of curried meat, cooked in
small pieces on a skewer.

stock
liquid containing the flavour and
nutrients obtained from
prolonged boiling of bones,
meat, fish or vegetables.

tarragon
a herb native to Europe and
parts of Asia. It has a delicate,
aromatic flavour and is often used
in French dressing and other
classical French sauces.

turmeric
the ground stem or root of
a plant of the ginger family.

watercress
a dark green spray of leaves which
grows in fresh flowing streams
of water; used in salads and for
garnishing meat dishes.

zest
thinly-pared rind from citrus
fruit such as lemons, limes,
oranges and grapefruit.

zucchini or courgette
small green marrow-like
vegetable.

Index

Figures in italics refer to illustrations

Avocado fancy salad bowl 66
Avocado prawn cocktail *13,* 14

Bacon, glazed baked 50
Banana ice cream 74
Banana rum mousse 74
Barbecue sauce 46
Bean salad, green 56
Beef, cold baked silverside 32, *33*
Beef, cold fillet *frontis,* 34
Beef curry 48, *49*
Beef Sate, barbecued 44, *45*
Beetroot salad 67
Berry milk shake 88

Cabbage salad 59
Carrot salad 54
Champagne and orange juice *85,* 86
Chicken, jellied 43
Chicken soup, chilled 26
Cider cup 88
Citrus green salad 64, *65*
Coffee, iced 88
Cole Slaw *53,* 55
Crab, dressed 36, *37*
Cream cheese, iced 83
Cucumber and pineapple hors
 d'oeuvre 15
Cucumber salad 66
Cucumber sauce 39

Fish, soused 40, *41*
Florida cocktail 16, *17*
French dressing 63
Fruits in syrup 72, *73*

Gazpacho 27
Grapefruit mousse 78
Greek salata 56, *57*
Green salad 62

Horseradish cream 34

Ice cream 71

Lemon cream soufflé 75

Lemon water ice, Italian 80, *81*

Mayonnaise 35
Melon ambrosia 72
Melon cocktail 14
Melon fruit cup 70
Melon with smoked ham 20, *21*
Mushroom bean salad 58
Mushroom liver pâté 22
Mushrooms Milord 16
Mushrooms vinaigrette 18

Orange, iced 86
Orange creams 79
Orange jelly /jello, quick 79
Orange milk shake 86
Oranges and grapes Grand Marnier
 76, *77*
Oyster cocktail 19

Pâté, mushroom liver 22
Pea salad 59
Peach chutney 51
Pineapple in sour cream 82
Pork oriental, cold loin of *29,* 31
Potato salad 60

Radish salad, cool 58
Raisin yellow rice 46

Salad, green 62
Salmon mousse 38
Scallops, barbecued spiced 47
Seafood salad 42
Sherry refresher 87
Strawberries, brandied *69,* 71

Tea, iced 87
Tomato avocado appetizer 23
Tomato juice, iced 26
Tomato parsley soup, chilled 24, *25*
Tomato salad 60, *61*
Tomato yoghurt soup, iced 24

Wine cooler 87